DEADLY SCORPION STING!

by Kevin Blake

Consultant: Professor Bryan Grieg Fry
Head of Venom Evolution Laboratory
School of Biological Sciences
University of Queensland, Australia

BEARPORT
PUBLISHING

New York, New York

Credits

Cover, © Protasov AN/Shutterstock; TOC, © Deep Desert Photography/Shutterstock; 4, © Thomas Marent/Minden Pictures; 5, © Wales News Service; 4–5, © Zhukov Oleg/Shutterstock; 6, © Vova Shevchuk/Shutterstock; 7T, © Stephen Dalton/Minden Pictures; 7B, © Alex Hyde/Minden Pictures; 8, © Alberto Ghizzi Panizza/Alamy; 9, © Piotr Naskrecki/Minden Pictures/Newscom; 10T, © Snowleopard1/iStock; 10BL, © prasom boonpong/Shutterstock; 10BR, © RealityImages/Shutterstock; 11, © All Around Photo/Shutterstock; 12, © Paul & Joyce Berquist/Animals Animals/AGE Fotostock; 13, © Sharon Moerdler-Green; 14, © Mónica Ortiz Uribe/Fronteras; 15T, © PhillipGua/iStock; 15B, © Jay Ondreicka/Shutterstock; 16, © Thibaud Despres/Animalli; 17T, © Annie Owen/robertharding/Alamy; 17B, © Sushil Chikane/ephotocorp/Alamy; 18, © Todd Bishop/GeekWire; 19T, © Federico Tovli/VWPics/Redux Pictures; 19B, © Enrique de la Osa/Reuters; 20, © PA Real Life; 21, © Iamyai/iStock; 22 (L to R), © IrinaK/Shutterstock, © Dennis W. Donohue/Shutterstock, and © Reality Images/Shutterstock.

Publisher: Kenn Goin
Senior Editor: Joyce Tavolacci
Creative Director: Spencer Brinker
Photo Researcher: Thomas Persano

Library of Congress Cataloging-in-Publication Data

Names: Blake, Kevin, 1978– author.
Title: Deadly scorpion sting! / by Kevin Blake ; consultant, Professor Bryan
   Grieg Fry, Head of Venom Evolution Laboratory, School of Biological
   Sciences, University of Queensland, Australia.
Description: New York, New York : Bearport Publishing, [2019] | Series:
   Envenomators | Includes bibliographical references
   and index.
Identifiers: LCCN 2018011087 (print) | LCCN 2018012093 (ebook) |
   ISBN 9781684027057 (ebook) | ISBN 9781684026593 (library)
Subjects: LCSH: Scorpions—Juvenile literature. | Scorpions—Venom—Juvenile
   literature.
Classification: LCC QL458.7 (ebook) | LCC QL458.7 .B59 2019 (print) |
   DDC 595.4/6—dc23
LC record available at https://lccn.loc.gov/2018011087

For more information, write to Bearport Publishing Company, Inc., 45 West 21st Street, Suite 3B, New York, New York 10010. Printed in the United States of America.

10 9 8 7 6 5 4 3 2 1

Contents

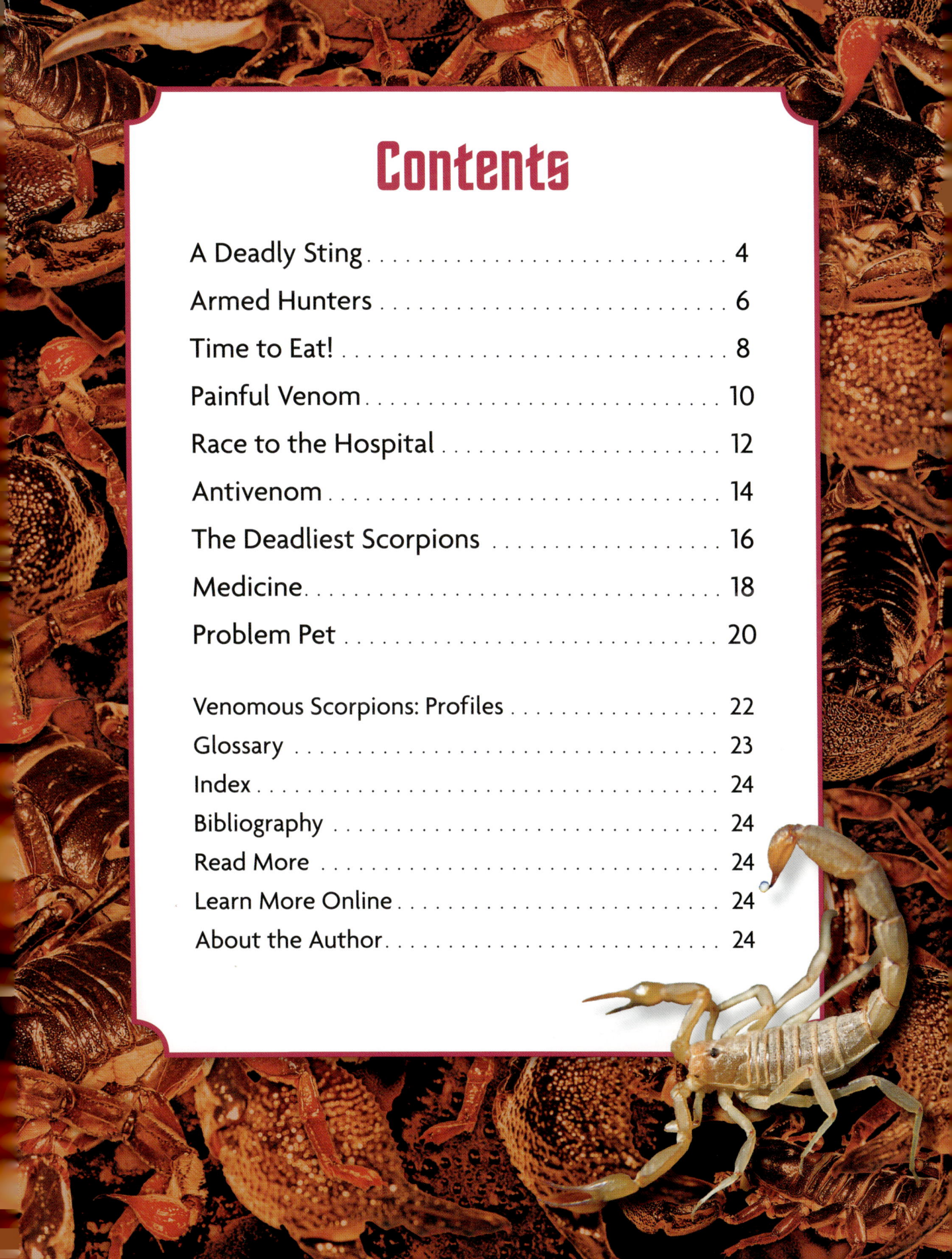

A Deadly Sting

Deep in the jungles of Thailand, Gareth Pike sprang out of bed one sunny morning in 2007. As he was getting dressed, he reached down to grab a pair of shorts off the floor. Suddenly, Gareth felt a horrible pain. "Something had stung me on the thumb," he said at the time. He quickly dropped his shorts and spotted a black scorpion scurrying away.

A black scorpion in Thailand

Scorpions kill more than 3,000 people each year. They live everywhere in the world except Antarctica.

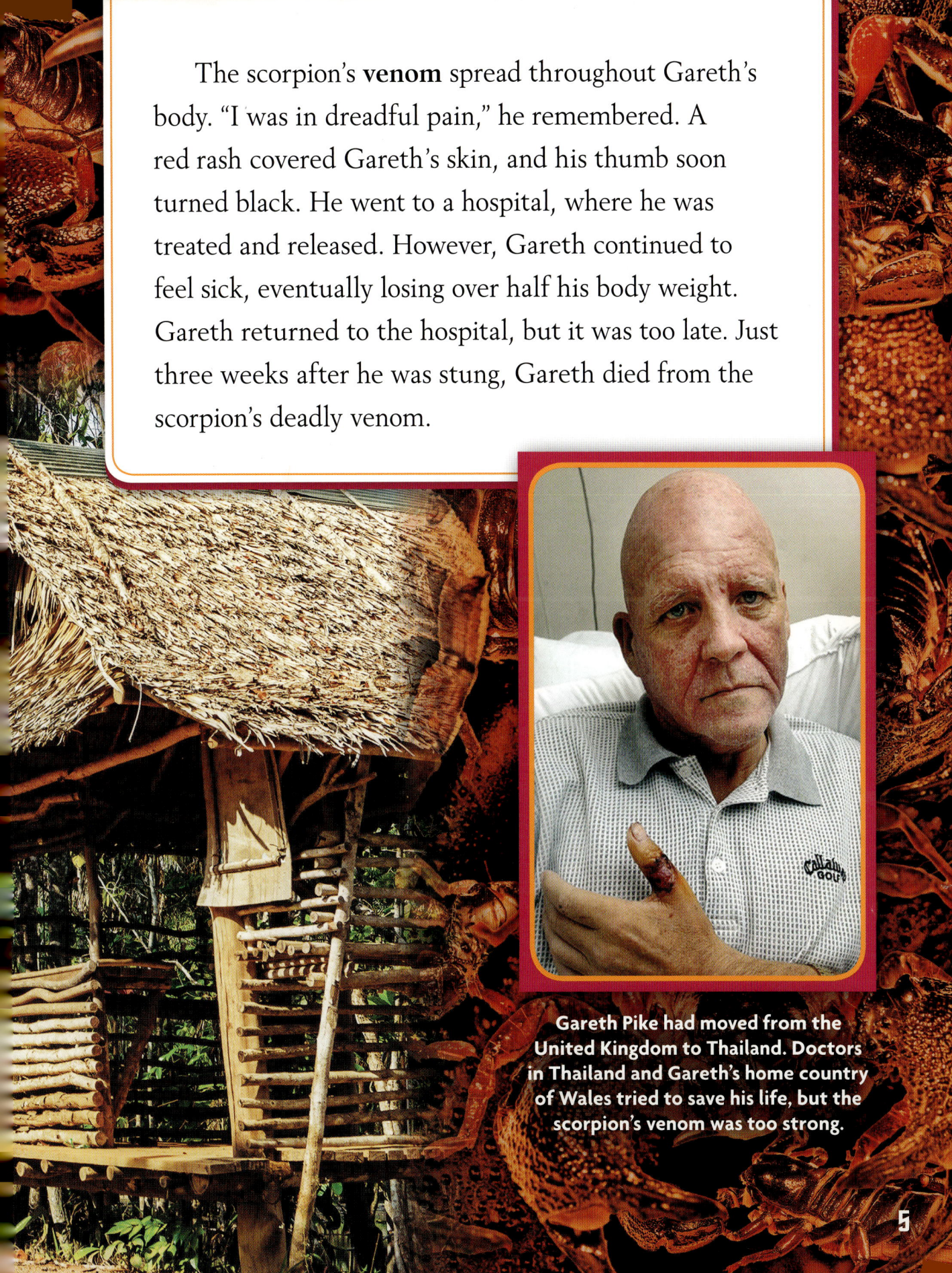

The scorpion's **venom** spread throughout Gareth's body. "I was in dreadful pain," he remembered. A red rash covered Gareth's skin, and his thumb soon turned black. He went to a hospital, where he was treated and released. However, Gareth continued to feel sick, eventually losing over half his body weight. Gareth returned to the hospital, but it was too late. Just three weeks after he was stung, Gareth died from the scorpion's deadly venom.

Gareth Pike had moved from the United Kingdom to Thailand. Doctors in Thailand and Gareth's home country of Wales tried to save his life, but the scorpion's venom was too strong.

Armed Hunters

Scorpions are small **arachnids** with large **pincers**. However, they have a second, more powerful weapon—venom. The venom is stored in a curved stinger at the end of their long tail. Scorpions only sting humans when they feel trapped or threatened. More often, scorpions use their venom to hunt **prey**, which includes insects, small lizards, and even other scorpions.

Stinger

Tail

Pincers

Scorpions are night hunters. They hide under rocks or plants, waiting for animals to cross their path. Once a scorpion **detects** prey, it uses its powerful pincers to grab the creature. Then the scorpion curls its tail over its back and stabs its prey with its venom-filled stinger.

This scorpion is about to use its stinger to send venom into its prey.

Stinger

Spider

Scorpions can have up to seven pairs of eyes, but they can't see very well. Their legs and pincers are covered with tiny hairs, which help them sense movement.

Time to Eat!

How does venom help the scorpion kill its prey? The venom acts very quickly to **paralyze** the animal. It sends chemical messages to the victim's brain and muscles. The chemicals cause the muscles to stop moving. The prey becomes frozen in place, like a statue.

Venom allows scorpions to eat animals much larger than themselves, such as this spider.

Once the prey is paralyzed, the scorpion prepares to eat its meal in a gut-churning way. First, it picks apart its prey with its pincers. Then, it covers the bits of meat with **digestive** juices to make them softer and easier to eat. Finally, the scorpion sucks up its gooey, liquid victim into its tiny mouth!

Cricket

Scorpions usually eat every couple of weeks, but some can survive a whole year without food.

Scorpions do not eat the hard outer parts of their prey.

Painful Venom

While all scorpions are venomous, only a few **species** have venom that's powerful enough to harm people. Even when the sting isn't dangerous, it's almost always painful. The venom causes **nerves** to send signals to the brain that spell instant agony! Dr. Leslie Boyer, the medical director of a poison center in Arizona, explains that even a tiny sting can send "shooting **sensations** up your arm" and leave a person screaming.

Of about 1,750 different species of scorpions, only about 25 can kill a human being.

Bark scorpion

Black scorpion

Fat-tailed scorpion

Scorpion venom has a special ingredient that makes it especially painful: **acid**. The acid can create a burning sensation that's like what a person feels after eating a very hot pepper. "When something is extremely hot, what we feel is pain," says Dr. Jie Zheng, a scientist who studies scorpion venom.

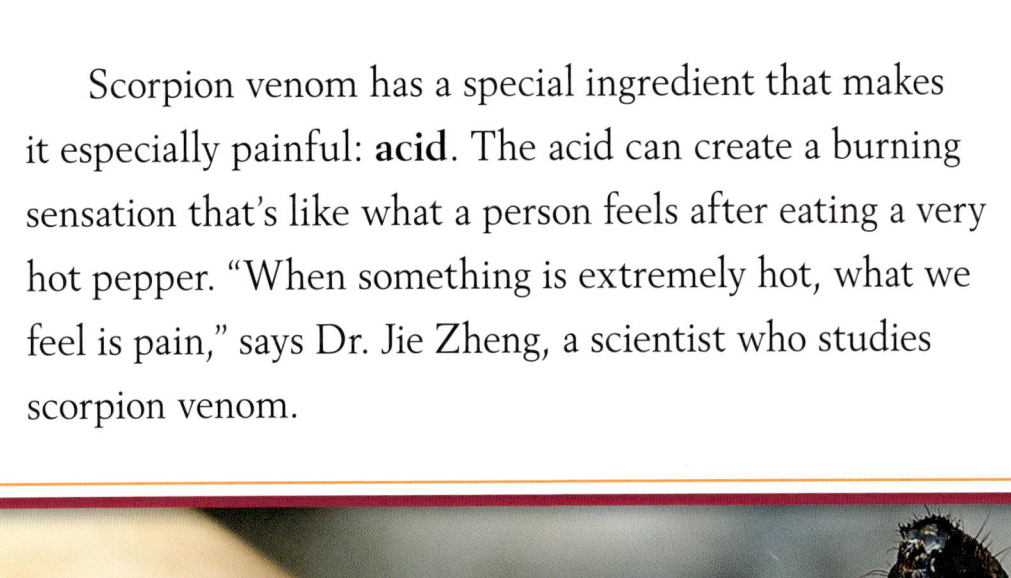

Scorpions should only be handled by experts.

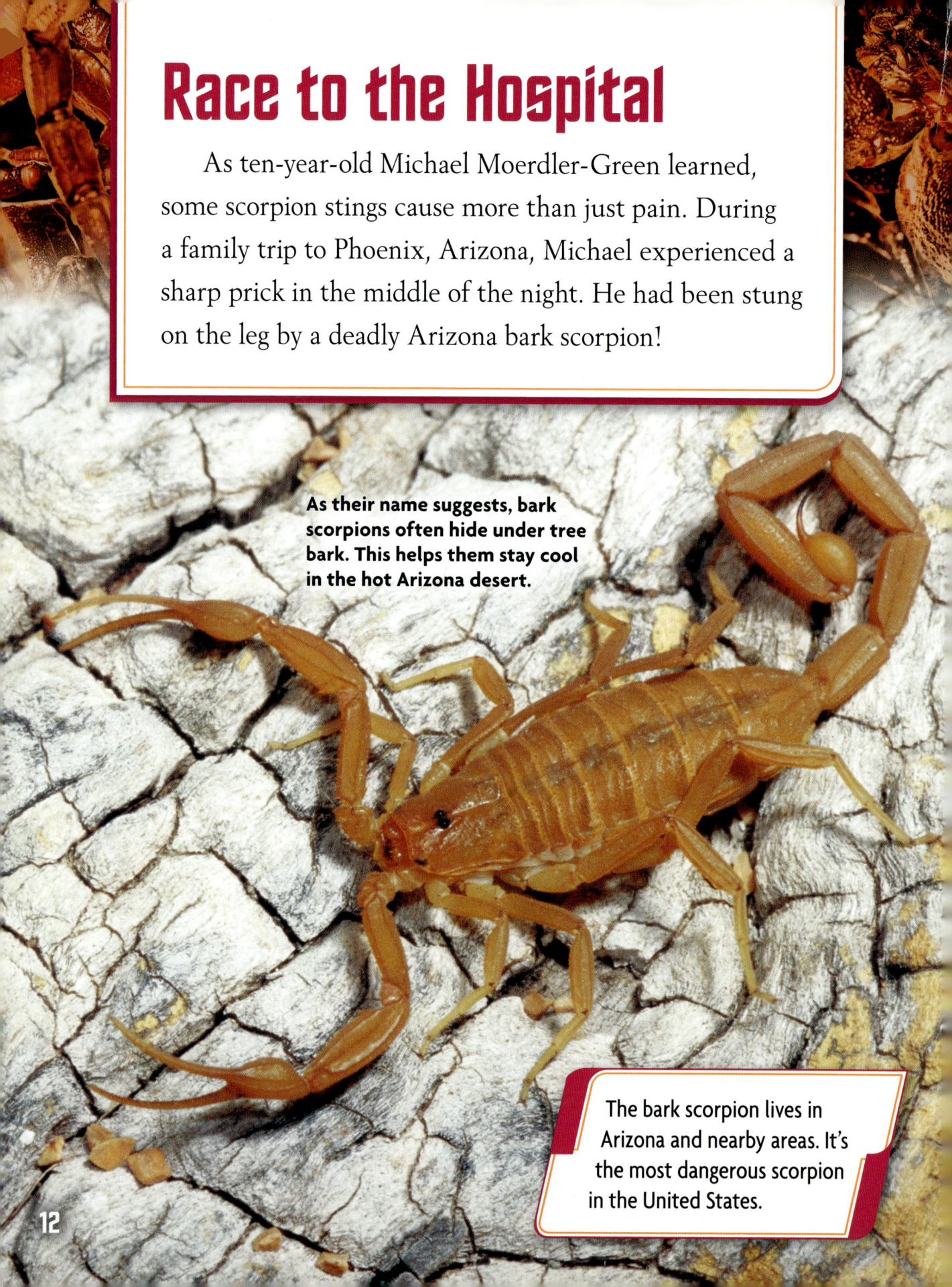

Race to the Hospital

As ten-year-old Michael Moerdler-Green learned, some scorpion stings cause more than just pain. During a family trip to Phoenix, Arizona, Michael experienced a sharp prick in the middle of the night. He had been stung on the leg by a deadly Arizona bark scorpion!

As their name suggests, bark scorpions often hide under tree bark. This helps them stay cool in the hot Arizona desert.

The bark scorpion lives in Arizona and nearby areas. It's the most dangerous scorpion in the United States.

Michael soon began feeling very strange. His body tingled. His eyes darted back and forth, and he couldn't stop them. Then Michael's arms and legs began to shake. His frightened parents rushed him to a nearby hospital. There, doctors gave Michael **antivenom** that had been specially designed to treat scorpion stings. The medicine worked, possibly saving Michael's life. The boy was able to leave the hospital one hour after receiving the treatment. "It was like a miracle," said Michael's relieved father.

Doctors at Phoenix Children's Hospital rushed to save the life of Michael Moerdler-Green (pictured above) after he was stung by an Arizona bark scorpion.

Antivenom

How do scientists create the antivenom that saved Michael's life? They use horses! At special farms, scientists **inject** small amounts of scorpion venom into a horse over a long period of time. The horse's blood naturally produces powerful **antibodies** to fight the poison. After the horse develops **immunity** to scorpion venom, scientists take some parts of the horse's blood and use it to make antivenom.

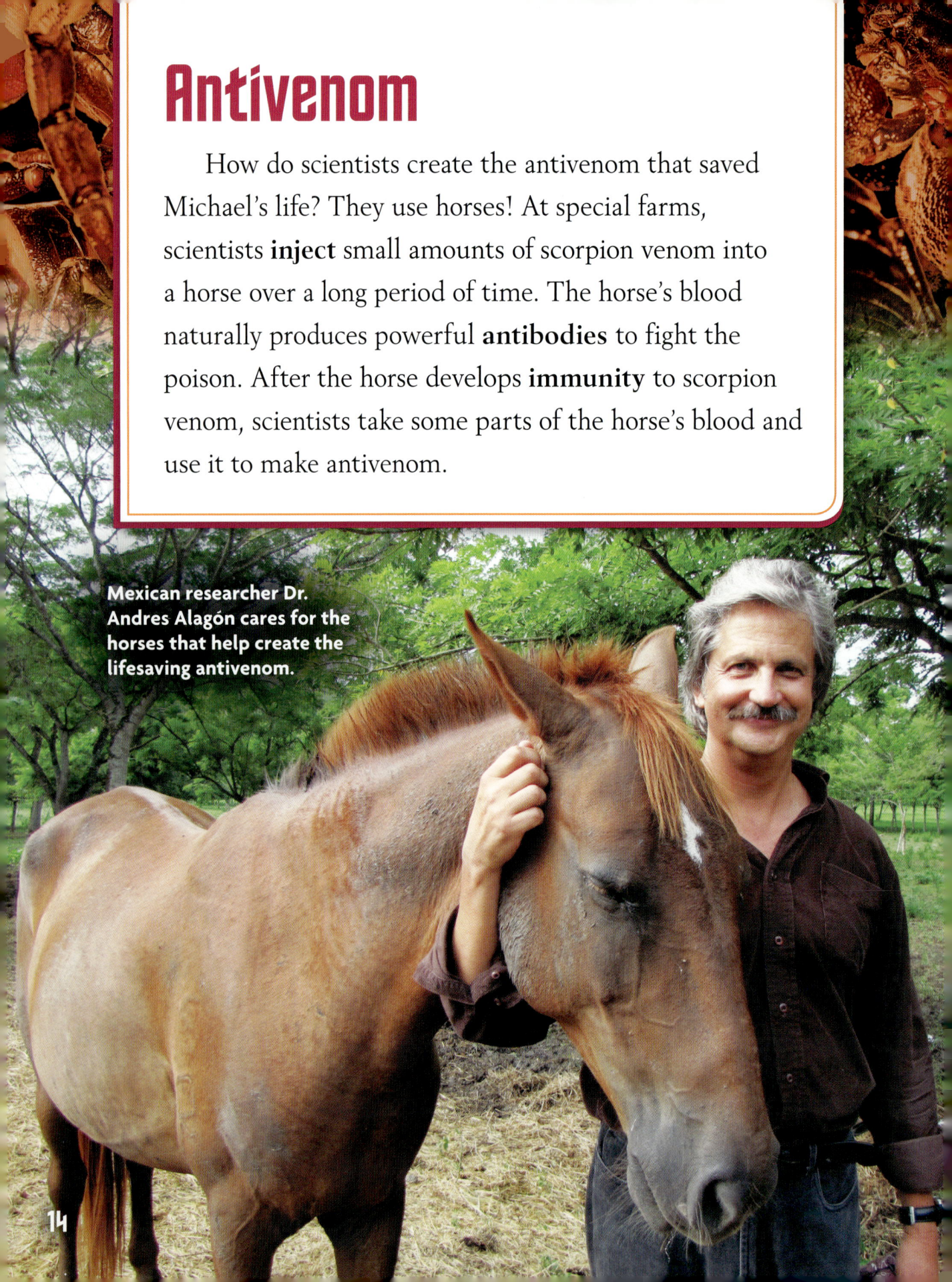

Mexican researcher Dr. Andres Alagón cares for the horses that help create the lifesaving antivenom.

Scorpion antivenom can help save lives—but it's not always readily available. When a bark scorpion stung six-month-old Daisy Moors in Oracle, Arizona, her parents were terrified. "The worst thing that could possibly happen was happening," Daisy's mother says. The baby was flown to the nearest hospital. On the helicopter ride, Daisy started shaking and throwing up. Unfortunately for Daisy and her family, the hospital did not have any antivenom. Daisy spent five days in the hospital, fighting for her life. Thankfully, she made a full recovery.

Helicopters are sometimes used to transport very sick people like baby Daisy from small towns to big hospitals.

Scorpion stings are most dangerous to babies and the elderly.

An Arizona bark scorpion like the one that stung Daisy Moors

15

The Deadliest Scorpions

It isn't just the bark scorpion that sends people to the hospital. The deathstalker scorpion is one of the most venomous scorpions in the world—it's also one of the fiercest. About the size of a human finger, the scorpion has an extremely painful sting. Its powerful venom can cause a person to have a heart attack. Over time, the scorpion's sting can also make the lungs fill with fluid, resulting in death.

The deathstalker scorpion lives in the deserts of Israel, Palestine, and Jordan. Its pincers are small and not very strong, which may explain why it needs such powerful venom to protect itself.

Another dangerous scorpion is the Indian red scorpion, which some scientists think is the most **lethal** in the world. No one is exactly sure how its venom works, only that it's deadly. Up to 40 percent of people—mostly children—who are stung by this scorpion die.

Many people walk around barefoot in South Asia. Often, they accidentally step on scorpions.

The Indian red scorpion is so **adaptable** to different temperatures that it can spend a night frozen solid, then thaw out in the morning and begin hunting again.

The Indian red scorpion lives in wet parts of India, Pakistan, and Sri Lanka.

Medicine

Scorpion venom is so powerful that scientists have been studying ways that it can help—rather than hurt—people. After years of research, Dr. Jim Olson discovered that components of the deathstalker's venom "stick" specifically to **cancer** cells while passing by healthy cells. This gave Dr. Olson an interesting idea.

Brain cancer researcher Dr. Jim Olson in his lab in Seattle, Washington

When Dr. Olson mixed the deathstalker's toxin with a special glowing dye and injected it into a patient, it showed **surgeons** where cancer is located in a person's body. "The scorpion toxin finds the cancer cells and drags the 'flashlight' into them and makes them glow brilliantly," Dr. Olson explained. This helps surgeons target and remove cancer cells during an **operation**.

A scientist carefully removes the venom from a scorpion to study it.

Scorpion venom has also been used to help treat other diseases, such as **Alzheimer's** and **diabetes**.

The venom is captured in a glass jar.

Problem Pet

With venom so powerful that it can fight deadly diseases, scorpions don't make the best pets. Dean Armstrong of Cambridge, England, found that out the hard way when his pet scorpion, Sue, stung him. Dean was in the worst pain of his life. "I thought I was going to die," he now says.

Scorpion venom works fast, so after a person has been stung, it's important to get medical attention quickly.

Dean Armstrong with another one of his unusual pets—a tarantula

Dean was lucky that he survived the scorpion sting—but just barely. He was sick for a long time and had to have major surgery. Doctors removed part of Dean's stomach and **pancreas**, which had been damaged by the scorpion's venom. "Still, I love scorpions," Dean admits. While scorpions are amazing animals, it's best to appreciate them from a safe distance.

Venomous Scorpions
— PROFILES —

	Arizona Bark Scorpion	**Deathstalker Scorpion**	**Indian Red Scorpion**

DESCRIPTION	The Arizona bark scorpion lives in and around the deserts of Arizona. These scorpions often climb trees or hide under objects or inside shoes. They are a light brown color.	Also known as the Israeli yellow scorpion, the deathstalker is actually tan colored to help it blend in with its sandy home. It lives in desert areas in North Africa and the Middle East.	In addition to being red in color, the Indian red scorpion can also be orange, brown, or gray. This species lives in forests and fields in India, Pakistan, and Sri Lanka.
LENGTH	About 3 inches (7.5 cm)	3.5 to 4.5 inches (9 to 11 cm)	About 2 inches (5 cm)
VENOM and Its Effects	A sting from the Arizona bark scorpion causes lots of pain, breathing problems, and sometimes muscle spasms. People say the sting can feel like electricity shooting through the body.	The deathstalker's venom contains many toxins, making its sting particularly painful and dangerous. The venom can cause paralysis and heart attacks.	While the Indian red scorpion may have the most powerful venom in the world, it doesn't sting as often as other scorpions. When it does strike, its painful sting can cause sweating, vomiting, difficulty breathing, and death.

Glossary

acid (ASS-id) a powerful chemical that can burn

adaptable (uh-DAPT-uh-bul) able to change to fit the environment

Alzheimer's (AHLTS-ahy-merz) an illness that causes memory loss and confusion

antibodies (AN-ti-bod-eez) chemicals in the blood that help fight diseases or poison

antivenom (an-tee-VEN-uhm) a medicine that blocks the effects of venom

arachnids (uh-RAK-nidz) the group of animals that includes scorpions

cancer (KAN-sur) a disease that destroys parts of the body

detects (di-TEKTS) finds or notices

diabetes (dye-uh-BEE-teez) a disease in which people have too much sugar in their blood

digestive (dye-JEST-iv) related to the breaking down of food

immunity (im-YOO-ni-tee) the body's ability to resist a disease or toxin

inject (in-JEKT) to force inside

lethal (LEE-thuhl) deadly

nerves (NURVZ) fibers that send messages from a person's brain to other body parts

operation (OP-uh-ray-shun) when a doctor cuts into someone's body to repair or remove a damaged or diseased part

pancreas (PAN-kree-us) a large gland in the body that helps it digest food

paralyze (PA-ruh-lize) to cause something to be unable to move

pincers (PIN-surs) the front claws of a scorpion

prey (PRAY) something that is hunted and attacked by something else

sensations (SEHN-say-shuns) feelings that make someone aware of something

species (SPEE-seez) groups of animals that share similar characteristics

surgeons (SUR-juhnz) doctors who perform operations

venom (VEN-uhm) toxic substances made by some animals

Index

Bibliography

Rabin, Roni Caryn. "An Experimental Drug Eases Poisonous Scorpion Stings in Children, a Study Finds." *The New York Times* (May 13, 2009).

Rock, Lucy. "How Scorpions Became an Unlikely Ally in the Fight Against Cancer." *The Observer* (November 1, 2015).

Read More

Franchino, Vicky. *Scorpions (Nature's Children).* New York: Scholastic (2015).

Lunis, Natalie. *Stinging Scorpions (No Backbone! The World of Invertebrates).* New York: Bearport (2009).

Learn More Online

To learn more about deadly scorpions, visit
www.bearportpublishing.com/Envenomators

About the Author

Kevin Blake lives in Providence, Rhode Island—thankfully far away from the deathstalker scorpion. He makes his home with his wife, Melissa, and their two children.